Notebook of Roses and Civilization

NICOLE BROSSARD

translated by Robert Majzels and Erín Moure

COACH HOUSE BOOKS TORONTO

Originally published in 2003 as *Cahier de roses et de civilisation*
by Éditions d'art le Sabord

Canada Council for the Arts Conseil des Arts du Canada

Canadä

This translation was funded by the Canada Council for the Arts Translation Grants program. The publisher would also like to thank, for their support, the Block Grant Programs of the Canada Council for the Arts and the Ontario Arts Council. We also acknowledge the Government of Canada through the Book Publishing Industry Development Program.

LIBRARY AND ARCHIVES CANADA CATALOGUING IN PUBLICATION

Brossard, Nicole, 1943-
[Cahier de roses & de civilisation. English]
Notebook of roses and civilization / Nicole Brossard ; translated by Robert Majzels and Erin Mouré. -- 1st ed.

Poems.
Translation of: Cahier de roses & de civilisation.
ISBN 978-1-55245-181-6

I. Majzels, Robert, 1950- II. Mouré, Erin, 1955- III. Title.

PS8503.R7C3413 2007   C841'.54   C2007-901568-9

Apparition of Objects

winter water blue melt backlit
life suddenly in thin chemise
steadfast
in questions and old silences

in the puzzle of proper nouns
and barking city: February
slow eyelashes that beckon to love
and spinning tops

foliage of word for word
gentleness that evades meaning
plunge into the dark
with metronome

crabs eels intestines
legs and antennae
destiny you said it
from memory
with a single verb

the thousand and one possibilities of the toe, the foot
the ankle
images in the subway glued to each other
faces pressed against the whys

the saliva the fingernails
it all goes beyond
adverbs and bones

the future the future
naked things design
audacity vertical

a woman in panties
half-spoken surrounded
by syntax and paintings

dark eyebrows
a starlet sings
an amphetamine clenched in her teeth

fire close to dying
at the edge of a forest
kiss that counts

someone standing
before an accident
of cars and fiction

under the eyelid:
time's measuring tape
dust in equilibrium

peoples and their signatures
their faces more alive
than crabs and pigeons in the shade
of cherry trees

poetry drawn back from daring
fiction if you ask me
hazelnut: image of an old
tomb with a squirrel

a photo repeated that sparks a taste
for pleasure with a grain of salt
on the tongue
a photo repeated
a stack of selves archived

big blue armchairs
their cloth arms worn down
by memory and odours
that intoxicate. Retina,
adjust your thoughts

emergency staircase on a slant
with slow blue flung at the sky
window and woman smiling

the rust the steel, broken panes
of America the colour of graffiti
then in slow motion: tulips appear
spinal cord
strange archives

on the iron rails
of a century the mud
of a day the immensity

Sombre: night flower
or calculated shadow
brief flame: hypothesis

Feinte speak reflection
seen through glasses
all words are ribbons

reading *lèvres* micro
i know the answer
poems that demand we open
the fire the heart: devour me

palace and ice
parentheses (duvet)
orange, epidermis
pillowcases
i beg of you: answer

birds pepper-coloured
a flight of silence with clouds
distant. I retrace my steps
touch here a woman's arm

tiny algae that enter
gastronomy
blue water imbued water
always another beginning

the lemon the martini the olive
all that amuses
then came night with its lampshades
describe the light
touch tomorrow

the immense everyday furled in the iris
a morning
of found orchids

Soft Link 1

It's fears slow and fascinating that enter life each morning at coffee time while she wonders if tomorrow there'll be war and brusquely as she does each morning slices bread and cheese. It's gestures of uncontrollable avidity that proliferate in the throng and its worldly febrility, its parquet fever on the trading floor and stage. It's hesitations, heart cries that crisscross broad avenues full of shade and dust that attract and make us think of our legs and elbows, our knees too when desire bumps and bounces words and feelings upward, it's simple things with prefixes like cyber or bio that hold thoughts fast, float them a moment till we believe them aquatic and marvellous. It's certainties that in tiny increments of dust and light are soon mixed with our tears. It's inexplicable feelings made of small hurts strung over long years and vast horizons, it's blues ideas that settle in where the happiness of existing threatens to take the breath away or to lodge itself in the throat like an instrument of fervour. It's glimmers of intoxications impossible to look at for long, thoughts so precise that engage us beyond shade and wind, far beyond crude words, so noisy so terribly close to silence that the world all around seems suddenly engulfed in high seas and continual rustling like the music in our heads that in one stroke of the bow dislodges all that resists torment. It's underlined passages, fragments of happiness that traverse the body and raise bridges all around because elsewhere and in the wild blue yonder they say there's euphoria. It's written down with bruises, abundance of life burst to fullness in a world and its niches of worn paths that lick at the shadow of bones.

Notebook of Roses and Civilization

poem to understand how
people bend
before an idea
their hair barely brushing the depth of silence

still some days still i
add bits onto the substance
of faces. Necklace of memory
and of animal torn from the abyss.
Seen from behind, necklace: verb to be.

once again the exact time the street
the cigarette we don't light
again the time the sex of lips
existence silence that deafens
another metamorphosis
arms open

sudden taste of the sea around the arms
with one toss of the lasso
a scent of life and sweetened peanuts

thousands of destinies sushi pasta deli
avid eyes averted
between the paragraphs and the eyelids
thousands of posters that stir
the night the sounds
of faces we might have caressed in thinking
future. Of the species
suddenly thousands of destinies out of the picture
a water that tastes of tears and bois bandé

it's Sunday: the soldiers are clean
shaven. There are children, girls
at the water's edge: animal corpse that goes
small log that the light carts off
with grasses, lilies
and cherries in bloom, olive trees
murmurs far off. Baobabs.

here people talk very loudly
blue toques, sunglasses
mobiles: words fast forgotten
things happen, right?
in swift cuts
things right to the blood

shadow of obelisk
you walked beneath a bridge
knot of questions
breathe deeply before the night
mix air and speech

the idea that there are
inconsolable centres
in the middle of the chest
while we keep on
coping
a notebook of roses
under the arm

thus
this vertigo with vowels glued to the intimate
to sleep and to the retina
all this time
roots that go on forever
old grief that runs through our hair

while caresses draw us close
to the source and to dawn
a fox's life you were saying

the colour of tears at the bottom
of a ravine
the heat of summer on the earlobe
it all feeds the senses:
madonnas that stoke the fever
an old translation of Virgil

when life runs
a tongue over the tongue
it transforms
distant sunflowers and suffering

then the world spreads out
digital and rewind
light crosses over
water's forgetting
the fluidity of selves:
récapitulons

to move on with *adieu* in the throat
tell it all to me with glimmers
scattershot of words becoming

groundswells that help us speak
we'd like to say goodbye to debris
with a logic of obscurity
caresses that make flight and desire
to ravish in a single lesson

nape nests of birds
essentials that come through the I
its arms open
to the false bottom of images
when life goes
from the tongue to the creatures of transparency

whatever the month or wound
the soft colour of afternoons
you plunge into
la lingua la lingua and its salty murmur

to the dawn add i am
in the middle
bite marks and certainty:
we all need
seashells and reality

the tongue rarely
approaches dawn
without a sob

you get carried away: repeatedly we
touch torso *torse*
the stability of night
in our chests
            the creatures

always in the past tense
the moon surprises our desires
how to touch?

there's black and the idea
of black a journey of hands
tremours as if the shadow were
about to penetrate the muscles
carve into flesh its own answers
on the subject of the universal

the word it touched it shattered
shadow. The face
although hurricane although
straight as a poplar
the word it made
its thin blade its horizon

PRECAUTIONS

1

humid and hot
the idea of a reed.
Repeat: it's night
later guess
what gives rise to the sensation
of easy languor. A void
at the level of life

2

furious words iron bar
line of light)
how to scream *dogs* in the midst
of a smell of burning
(of tires
of night

3

from eyelash to wound
life has to lie flat
don't you think
between us and the mirrors

4

humidity in the eyes
it concerns us
such an old mystery
a sky of animals
brume with signatures that wander

SUGGESTIONS HEAVY-HEARTED

1

the idea of balancing on the tip of an I
suspended
by the feverish joys of July
or salivating before the dark
of a present filled with
whys that stream through thoughts

2

then give me the pleasure
of tracing words impossible to tear holes in
go back through the course of time
between dialogues don't waver

3

repeat: memory
hold fast. The tongue
it calls
on us, on everything
curls up everywhere to feed
on silence

4

an idea of absolute
carried off in a word in a blast
of wind
ask your question

SMOOTH HORIZON OF THE VERB LOVE

1

an urban image from the eighties
when we hung out at Chez Madame Arthur
and at the back of the room
women wrapped their arms around
nights of ink and dawn

2

calendar of murmurs
vague caresses about the planet and its water
we could have confused words
but there were doors open
confetti in the midst of darkness
gentle ways
to swoon in a corner with she who
put her tongue in my mouth

3

focus on yes, on the woman's
eyelids
caress not silence not word
focus beyond. Hold me back

RUSTLING AND PUNCTUATION

1

the world we're winded
wound-up passion
unfurling under the tongue

2

a street name a shadow that floats
glued like a weekday
to the dust
old refuge: use the familiar

3

often that's happiness
say i love you or sleepless night
colours that precede
the iodine of words
torment of punctuation

4

turn your head to the right side
of the horizon and water
this is Montréal cheek to cheek
embedding in the tongue
a scent of enigma, a link

EVERY ARDOUR

1

beware of words that blur
of summer heat that unfurls
like an ocean over the species

2

thus we'll leave
without remembering
verbs in their time
that brought us closer
to mirrors and rapture

3

since immensity seeks
to take on another form
imagine the speed of the murmur
the noisy surging of old intentions
this great yes risen
from the depth of memory

4

if the whole body is bent over
what respite if the body
kneels breaks surface
at the hour of bedsheets or ink

IT'S LIVELY

1

fountain/fossil: wouldn't you rather
roll tomorrow
off the tip of the tongue
restart reality break day

2

it's lively you might say
a colour that doesn't
make sense it's so real that we think
riot of genes dashing madly
in broad daylight toward the origin

3

you sleep a bit of DNA in your silence
you sleep up close to the word dissect
thinking: we'll go
a great shout in our chests
try out our parachutes

wooden benches turned toward nature
disasters and our smiles
copper and iron benches
tangled in our goodbyes:
Figure 1 and Figure 2
follow on notes to the self

one more car horn in the night
arms of lovers and twenty-first century
Soho: you lean from your window
the alphabet, other chasms
the self whirls the self becomes
fragile filament of presence
in the face of tomorrow
still i take notes in roman numerals
I II III IV V VI VII VIII IX X and so on

maternité hangs from a thread
bound only by a wavelength
ribbon the colour of living blood
maternité odour of eternity

all this that wasn't a story
to begin again
it's the whole being that yields marvellously

end of a dream at the ends of the earth
war took
root in the morning dew
rip through the wind, all the arrows

even if we add i
so who made this picture
with no eye and a pen
where are you headed your back in that sweater
summer on your shoulder
without the weight of bones?

all the dreams we don't carry away
blur in the night like fans
kites unimaginable enigmas
we have to breathe

in the wake of the pen: scent of dusk
the word wound because of the fragility
of irises
of white cosmos and of night that falls
in the midst of road incidents
toys that suddenly displace the horizon:
cross here

joyful ribbon of old forests
held by the hair
or urban caress: choose wisely
your wound, the hotel
don't rave
not yet go further

one evening going all the way to the tip
of my fingers i revive
suddenly silence
on the far side of reality who's there?
Touch anyway.

the idea of cortège, we were just looking
for spaces. Comfortable languor
the better to plunge
into the imperfect tense
of a grammar in the grip of speed
amidst its own fragments
of silence and nostalgia

in mid-garden it seemed
you wanted to go
into nature with a bone
to walk in the universe
the same intention lurking for
centuries in your thoughts

ferociously nomadic: life
its rare words stacked in the imagination like
multicoloured soaps, all scent
and high ecstasy
depending on whether a clock or tenacious light
moves thoughts

the c of cerise that is not yet a comma
between you and me and this foretaste of translation
traced like an arc in the mouth
an obsessive curve that could look like
your belly, or those typos found
in books
noise of goodbye or movement of the lips
ardour

the poem can't lose its momentum
make you suddenly turn around
as if the sea
were about to surge up at your back
in pages of foam and foment

as if the sea
with its syllables of water could
transpose death help you
to make slow curves in time

when we're struggling to hang on to solutions
why must we suddenly
stretch a part of our being toward fiction
step back from words just as we emerge from
the time of scars

don't forget to turn the page
with a light hand each time
so that the shadow doesn't touch
the front of solitude

today, there are neither insects
nor rain, just roots
along the eyelashes
rumours of snow and alphabets

but life! One day i'll speak
of life with revived
brain haunted
by numbers and eternity
i'll enter the present
eyes riveted to
every warning

A little more. Talk of drawers
and the future. Of a truce in the war
stuck to science
talk of nudity, of bones
of poetry that often
gathers in the voice
liqueurs and the silence of bays

from tomorrow onward i am
plunged into the unthinkable
immense dawn
nobody and yet
au revoir perhaps
the universe is strikingly beautiful
night shadow or dust

renaissance ideas
while inventing
future at the nape of the neck
the lightness of the luminous shores
all this that knocks
on the root of the sky. Above all calculate
the background noise of characters

in what year did we forget
time the idea of our muscles wild and carnal
in what year
did you turn back
to the water
to the cycle of shadows?

but on the other hand who gains from
reading a landscape
and likewise where does the echo go
the infinite tenderness of cliché
when we dream
our hand at rest
on the genitals
so that only
a spellbound tongue takes flight

it’s an old word full
of roots and obstacles
that heads straight
for our mouths to find refuge.
Answer:
– Too much shadow

a mere nothing torments
page two: happiness is easy
salt or silence. On the other hand
life spits out the universal
at each twig of presence
tosses its eggs above the chasm
salt or silence lay down
the present along inebriate shores

from each side of existence
draw your own leaps of light
if that makes sense
head into the din without renouncing
the harsh wind that instinctively writes its name
in your every gesture

i arrive at this page burning.
others use the word light
to shake up reality. Let's see
if standing up you grab tomorrow naked
out of order

solitude's doing fine
you in the language thinking of tomorrow
you're still too close to
abstract words
to see it coming the satin the salt air
the war the ancient me

Soft Link 2

But there's outside, the cold the heat the violence doubled over in pain in a real bind at the edge of city and forest, there's outside and it's worse each time as there's traffic of weapons, traders of women and children, white-shirted men who manipulate our genes and cells like so much merchandise. And it seems to me we have to be in the world often and in a flash traverse all the to-and-fro of desire, go from there to long ago or tomorrow like a chamois on a windshield swiping across the back of the universe. But there's outside and you might say as a result that the world's hard to take despite the December luminosity of tropical breezes. Inside, words let us invent, weave cords strong enough to hang by our wrists and help balance the body. Outside there's outside with horizons, shortcuts, strange fears reborn in the body and its desire to take flight, but there's outside like hunting with prey, pellets, kingdoms, identities hidden under clothes; there are cemeteries, discos, security zones, war measures. Outside if we touch the living face of things, the beautiful face all spun with life easily unfurls its roses, its luminous whites that traverse children's voices, their laughing arms. But there's outside where the living face of suffering never shows. So you fall asleep on the name of public things forgetting the darkness that runs easily through life, the blur in the eyes that gathers bones north of the forehead like fruits, toys, words with their angled knees and elbows and the tree nuts that parade in answer or that smash and transform shadow words those that race the pulse and modulate again and again the tremours of beasts with shivers. But there's outside there's the duration of wandering. Outside there's the knowing dawn.

Blue Float of Days

you always think it's fine
to count the words. Then you go quiet
before all the deletions
and denouements, you
plunge into silence toward its underlying
truth quick it'll have resurfaced
like an insect in the pool

depending on the angle of sofa or street
from the corner of the eye, the screen or calendar
you can't bear to watch them
those conical women blue shadows
blinded by men with eyes
of Kalashnikovs and bloody verse
depending on the angle
goodbye humanity the heart fires
point blank

in a time blue and easy
when the light is slow
and ties urgent knots
with shadow and catastrophe
you say we need rain
rain and even more night
than the abyss can rein in
or the silence of people of tenderness

sun flanked by salt and solitude
i watch life pass by, two beings in the flesh
a yellow Jag, a century of raving
of such violent feeling
at the foot of pages and monuments

a gathering of *everywhere* and *elsewhere*
rooted in consciousness
like spines on edge amidst
inexplicable tensions
a taste for universe and birth grazing the lips
fervours so strong we're mere debris)
the heart
summer evenings along the coasts of Maine
(brise de mer

what’s there to say lying down in civilization
and its vertiginous equations
when the night lets fly its missiles
ardent things grazing the lips

on the bent back of light
nothing's banal
life starts again
the wind has broad shoulders
electrifies thoughts skin
and the rosy thing with the rare taste of
utopia and recitation
while night plays dead
and all that's needed
on the bent back of the tongue

it’s one of those things
you keep starting over
in the chest
it’s my body we’ll say
think of the pleasure of that first coffee
and of breathing
let’s draw the line
on time draw the line
impulsively every day
on death and distant
let’s be what appears every day

walls there are walls
encircled by transparency
we'd be vultures
turned around awaiting the turn of who
who'd have believed it
walls, there are walls
in our bones
walls in ruins that lament

yesterday again i thought of the word orange
the words cerise, olive, words we stick in our mouths
but skull was the word that surged up
then chalkscratch and childhood
then heart shoulder and knee no commas
episodes to placate desire maybe
to watch the ocean and our cells contend
in the light
until again and proximity of shoulder
yesterday still it could all be read

slow you want it slow
of course in the run of each phrase
as it runs off the tongue runs out of intention
with each fierce embrace you want
shadowy meanings shared
with the tongue only
in the course of words of their apparition
fertile in the mouth you can
cross the continent
devour it all there tranquil

in real torment
it's easy and enough
to level all thoughts and await
a tropical bird or siren's voice
a surge impossible to narrate
in the centre of silence that would do harm
to torment

another pause and there'll be
some blue
the eyes' good luck before
the blue float of days

in time by and large
all these things lie upstream of
thought you notice them at the fall
of day in the gulf
or all along the coast with its bays
its Manhattan, its capes, almandine Cuba,
butterfly Guadeloupe and all that lives
with gaps here and there of humanity
or of happiness you might say kite
high over the ocean
sun apeak deep in us who watch it
passionately go under

the phrase starts with maybe
you turn in circles to understand it
then it unwinds
as continuous coastline
an America pressed up against thoughts like a fjord
knot of myths left hanging
at the hour of limitless lives without orchid
at the hour of the scent of books begun again

don't forget
deep in the belly
there are minerals that crumble away
like packets of light
vital planets. Today
you're not sombre

all these months spent
gazing at the palms from below
the birth of the scent of jasmine
all this time spent
seeking the twilight zone at the edge of *l'univers*
yes from below its birth
when the head is plunged
into a world of voices
and the heart swathed in its excesses of reality

finally in the midst of a living tongue
well irrigated i'll have
such momentum at my fingertips
we could call it
theatre with petals
humanity's days numbered
or apparition of objects
then come the conflagrations

Soft Link 3

It's names of places, cities, climates that haunt. Characters. Clear mornings, a fine rain that falls all day, rare images from elsewhere and America, two natural disasters that make us close ranks amid corpses, it's quiet or violet acts, mortars, ice cubes in glasses at cocktail hour, noise of dishes or a slight stutter that momentarily torments, a slap, kiss, it's names of cities like Venice or Reading, Tongue and Pueblo, names of characters Fabrice Laure or Emma. Words honed over years and novels, words we spoke with halting breath laughing spitting sucking an olive, verbs we add to the pleasure of lips, to success, to sure death. It's words like cheek or knee and still others further than we can see that leave us teetering on the edge of the abyss, to stretch like cats in morning it's words that keep us up till dawn or make us flag down a cab on a weekday night when the city's asleep before midnight and solitude is caught like an abscess in the jaw. It's words spoken from memory, in envy or pride often words uttered with love while laying our hands behind the head or pouring a glass of port. It's words whose etymology must be sought, then projected on a wall of sound so the cries of pain and sighs of pleasure that wander in dreams and documents lay siege to the mysterious darkness of the heart. It's words like bay, hill, *wadi, via, rue, stradă,* dispersed through the dictionary between flamboyancies and neons, burial mounds and forests. It's words arms of the sea, ensembles of sense that claw or *soft* at our chest, cold shivers rivulets and fear abrupt in the back while we try to fissure the smooth time of the future with trenchant quotations. It's words that swallow fire and life, who knows now if they're Latin French Italian Sanskrit Mandarin Galician Arab or English, if they conceal a number an animal or old anguishes impatient to shoot up before our very eyes like cloned shadows replete with light and great myths.

ACKNOWLEDGEMENTS

The author wishes to thank the Canada Council for the Arts for funding this translation, and also to acknowledge the pleasure and inspiration that come from sharing with Erín Moure and Robert Majzels questions about the auras and colours of words in our mutual languages.

The translators wish to thank Oana Avasilichioaei for her readings and suggestions at various points in the translation, Claire Huot for her sharp eye and flexible tongue, and Nicole Brossard for her generous lifelines.

ABOUT THE AUTHOR

Nicole Brossard was born in Montreal in 1943. Since 1965, she has published more than thirty books, including *Museum of Bone and Water, The Aerial Letter and Mauve Desert*. In recognition of her contributions to the revitalization of francophone poetry in Quebec, Brossard has twice been awarded the Governor General's Award for Poetry, first in 1974 and again ten years later. In 1965, she co-founded the literary periodical *La barre du jour* and, in 1976, the feminist journal *Les têtes de pioche*. That same year, she co-directed the movie *Some American Feminists*. She was also awarded the Prix Athanase-David, Quebec's highest literary distinction. In 2006, she won the Canada Council's prestigious Molson Prize for lifetime achievement. Her books have been translated into English, Spanish and Japanese. She lives in Montreal.

ABOUT THE TRANSLATORS

Robert Majzels is a novelist, poet, playwright and translator. He is the author of the full-length play *This Night the Kapo* (Playwrights Canada Press), and four novels, most recently *Apikoros Sleuth* (The Mercury Press, 2004) and *The Humbugs Diet*, forthcoming also from The Mercury Press in October 2007.

Erín Moure is a poet and a translator from French, Galician, Portuguese and Spanish. Her most recent book of poetry is *O Cadoiro* (Anansi, 2007), and her translation from Galician of Chus Pato's *Charenton* will appear in 2007 from Shearsman Books (UK and US) and BuschekBooks (Canada).

Typeset in Laurentian with Pirouette
Printed and bound at the Coach House on bpNichol Lane

Edited by Alana Wilcox
Designed by Stan Bevington
Cover photograph
Sala Alejo Carpentier, Gran Teatro de la Habana,
2000 © Robert Polidori

Coach House Books
401 Huron Street on bpNichol Lane
Toronto Ontario M5S 2G5

416 979 2217
800 367 6360

mail@chbooks.com
www.chbooks.com